DEMCO

Everything You Need to Know About

Epilepsy

Epilepsy can cause major convulsions—uncontrollable, often violent seizures.

Everything You Need to Know About

Epilepsy

Patricia Emanuele, R.N.

The Rosen Publishing Group, Inc.
New York

The author wishes to thank Brenda Simmons and the Epilepsy Foundation of America for their help in making this book possible, Eileen Valinoti for editorial guidance, and Vanessa Emanuele and my friends and family for encouragement.

Published in 2000 by The Rosen Publishing Group, Inc.
29 East 21st Street, New York, NY 10010

Library of Congress Cataloging-in-Publication Data

Emanuele, Patricia.
    Everything you need to know about epilepsy / Patricia Emanuele.
      p. cm. — (The need to know library)
    Includes bibliographical references and index.
    Summary: Discusses the history of epilepsy, its diagnosis, treatment, and special concerns for teenagers who must cope with this condition.
    ISBN 0-8239-3161-7
    1. Epilepsy—Juvenile literature. [1. Epilepsy. 2. Diseases.] I. Title. II. Series.

RC372.2 .E46 2000
616.8'53—dc21

                  99-088769

Manufactured in the United States of America

Contents

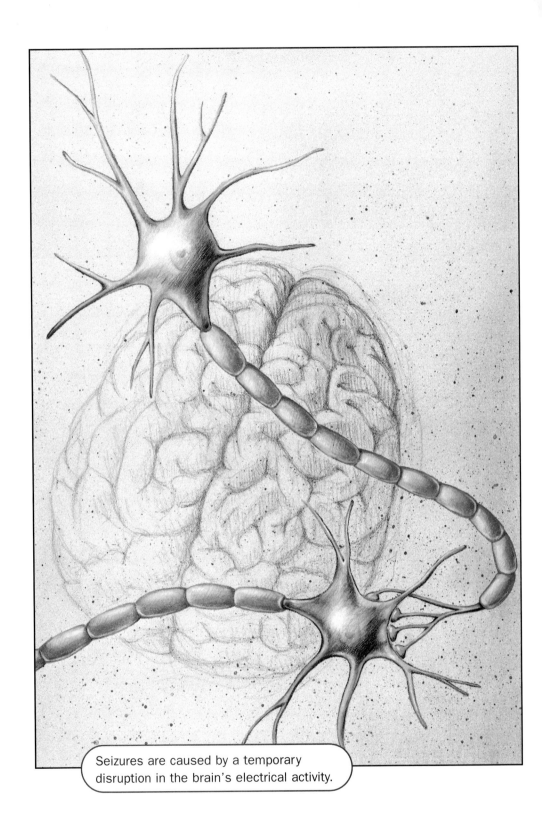

Seizures are caused by a temporary disruption in the brain's electrical activity.

Chapter One | Epilepsy and Seizures

The brain is the body's computer. It takes in information, stores and retrieves it, and controls all the body's functions. The brain is a three-pound spongelike mass, with billions of neurons (in the form of brain cells) and blood vessels contained within it. The hard shell of the skull protects it.

Each brain cell has a specific job and is located in a specific region of the brain. Each region deals with a distinct body function, such as breathing, speech, memory, or movement. Brain cells constantly discharge electrical energy by sending signals through the body in an orderly fashion.

If signals are sent too rapidly or at an irregular rate, a seizure will occur. A seizure is any temporary disruption in the electrical activity of the brain. Seizures cause changes in a person's movement or behavior. They can produce major convulsions—uncontrollable, often violent muscle movements—or minor twinges and other strange sensations. People can have temporary disturbances in the brain cells without any changes in movement or behavior. These people are not having seizures. Seizures are sometimes called fits, spells, convulsions, and attacks.

What Is Epilepsy?

The word "epilepsy" comes from a Greek word meaning "to seize" or "to attack." Epilepsy is a brain disorder that causes seizures, and it is sometimes referred to as a seizure disorder. Seizures are considered a symptom of epilepsy, just as a sore throat may be considered a symptom of a cold. During a seizure, out-of-control brain cells are producing electricity that attacks normal brain cells and affects how you feel, think, or act. Epileptic seizures can vary in how long they last, how frequently they occur, and when they occur. Each person with epilepsy has a different seizure pattern.

If a person has seizures, he or she does not necessarily have epilepsy. Seizures can occur because of fever, drug withdrawal, a severe allergic reaction, or lack of oxygen to the brain, for example. These seizures are not considered epilepsy. Having a single seizure does not mean a person has epilepsy either. A person is considered to have epilepsy after having two or more seizures not caused by fever, illness, or any other medical reason.

What Are Seizures?

There are at least thirty different types of seizures. The types of seizures differ depending on what region of the brain they affect. A seizure can affect any of the senses or cause a part of the body to move by itself. It can also cause changes in behavior.

A seizure can be nothing more than a brief staring spell or the sudden occurrence of a strange sensation, such as an unusual smell or funny feeling. Other types of seizures can cause a person to fall to the ground as if he or she has fainted. Some types of seizures produce convulsions, during which the entire body becomes stiff and shakes uncontrollably, and the person salivates. These seizures can look frightening to someone who does not know what is happening. They are not painful, however, and people who experience this type of seizure do not remember it afterward. They only know what a seizure is like from what other people tell them.

Types of Seizures

Seizures are described as either partial or generalized, depending on the part of the brain that is affected and how wide an area of the brain becomes seized by disorderly electrical activity of the brain cells. When one specific part of the brain is affected, the seizure is partial.

There are simple partial and complex partial seizures. A limb may jerk involuntarily during a partial seizure. A person having a simple partial seizure is aware of it happening. With complex partial seizures, a person may have an odd feeling or exhibit strange behavior, such as picking at clothing or wandering aimlessly. People usually do not remember having complex partial seizures.

Sometimes the brain cell activity that causes a partial seizure spreads to the rest of the brain. When the whole brain is affected, a generalized seizure occurs. Generalized seizures, which are somewhat less common than partial seizures, may be brief staring spells, major muscle movements, or full convulsions. Two common types of generalized seizures are absence (petit mal) and tonic-clonic (grand mal) seizures.

During an absence seizure, a person appears to be daydreaming and may have mouth, eye, or limb movements. The person does not answer when called; when the brief episode ends, he or she immediately resumes activity. Several absence seizures can occur in a day. They are common in children and are often outgrown.

During a tonic-clonic seizure, the person falls and loses consciousness. These seizures progress in two main phases. First is the tonic phase, in which the body stiffens and breathing slows or stops. The clonic phase follows, with severe muscle jerking, drooling, and possible loss of bowel or bladder control. Gradually, regular breathing returns and the person regains consciousness.

People may have more than one type of seizure. Correctly identifying the type of seizures a person has helps doctors decide the right treatment for that person.

Seizures are not contagious—you can't "catch" them from others. Most of the time, despite doctors' efforts, no cause is found for seizures. In some cases, though, doctors do find the cause and can eventually stop the seizures.

Causes of Epilepsy

The cause of epilepsy is unknown in most cases, but head injuries are one common cause. A serious blow to the head can injure brain cells. If brain cells temporarily shut down, or if electrical activity between them is interrupted, a concussion may occur. A concussion is a serious brain injury resulting from a violent blow. It can cause memory loss, dizziness, numbness, headache, disorientation, slurred speech, or unusual behavior. A concussion does not necessarily involve loss of consciousness. Concussions can sometimes cause seizures.

In some cases, if a newborn does not get enough oxygen during birth, the delicate electrical system in the brain may be damaged, leading to seizures. Other causes of seizures include brain tumors, genetic conditions, lead poisoning, problems in brain development before birth, and infections that affect the brain, such as meningitis and encephalitis.

Jon, fifteen, gets poor grades, and his progress reports always say that he is "capable of doing better." He eats well, gets enough sleep and exercise, and gets along fairly well with his family.

11

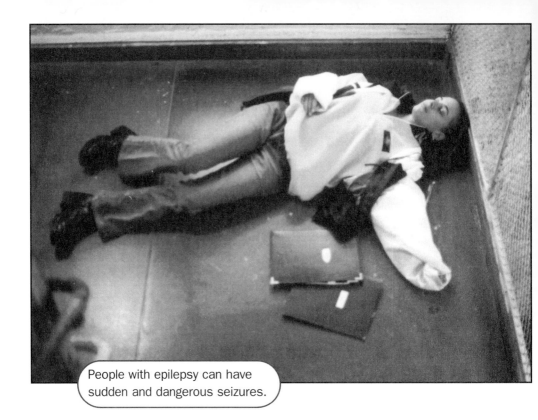

People with epilepsy can have sudden and dangerous seizures.

Sometimes Jon's teacher asks him a question and he just stares into space. The teacher thinks Jon isn't paying attention. When he finally responds, Jon says he didn't hear the question. Jon is having a seizure each time this happens, but no one knows it, not even Jon himself.

One day, Oliver, a senior, was going down the stairs at school when he saw Beth lying on the landing. She was very stiff and her eyes had rolled back up into her head. Soon her whole body started shaking. Then after a minute or two, she looked like she had fallen asleep. There was saliva trickling from her mouth. Beth had just had a seizure.

Chapter Two

A Historical Perspective

It is scary to learn that you have epilepsy. No one likes to have anything "wrong" with them—especially teens. There are many fears and misconceptions about epilepsy. Some people may believe certain myths about epilepsy: that it is a sign of mental illness or mental retardation, that it means you are possessed by evil spirits, or that it is contagious. None of these statements is true.

Epilepsy has been around for centuries. However, there are still many myths, stigmas (shameful associations), and misunderstandings about what it is, what causes it, and what people who have epilepsy are like. In the past, in many societies, people with epilepsy were thought to be possessed by demons and were often burned at the stake. Other societies

Epilepsy is much better understood today than it was in the past.

thought that people with epilepsy had inferior or weak minds. People with epilepsy were discriminated against, abused, and even punished for having seizures. Fear and lack of understanding help maintain old, incorrect attitudes.

Over the years we have learned much about the brain and why some seizures occur, and we have made progress in the diagnosis and treatment of epilepsy. Public attitudes have changed over the years, but many people still do not understand the condition and may believe old myths about it. If you or someone you know has epilepsy, knowing the facts can help lessen the fears. There is no reason to be ashamed about having epilepsy.

Myths and Misconceptions

People have had epilepsy throughout history, and there have always been misunderstandings about it. In the seventeenth century, people believed that epilepsy was caused by demons. Then it was thought to be contagious. At one time, people believed that masturbation caused seizures, and many men who had seizures were castrated to stop them from masturbating.

Public attitudes, and even laws, were cruel to those who had epilepsy. At one time, people with epilepsy were locked up with the mentally ill and were considered harmful. Some were discouraged from attending school or getting married, and prevented from having children.

Medical discoveries have helped our understanding of epilepsy. In England in the late 1800s, Dr. Hughlings Jackson discovered that specific regions of the brain control specific parts of the body. Tests that help us understand the brain have evolved over time. The discovery of X rays in 1895 helped to show a picture of the brain. In the 1930s, the electroencephalogram, or EEG, was introduced. This test measures the electrical activity in the brain. Computerized tomography (CT) was first used in 1973. This form of testing, also called a CAT scan, provides a three-dimensional image of the brain. Today there are even more technologies for examining the brain.

Measuring and testing the brain's functions helps medical professionals to understand the effects of epilepsy, but it does not always reveal the cause. We know that there are many causes of epilepsy, but in about 70 percent of cases, the cause is not known.

At one time, people with epilepsy were thought to have low intelligence or to be mentally incompetent or retarded. We now know that this is not true. Although it is possible for people with mental disabilities to also have epilepsy, the two conditions are separate and unrelated. In most cases, people with epilepsy are just as intelligent and mentally able as those without epilepsy. Some people with epilepsy are above average in intelligence and some are below, just like those without epilepsy. It is true, however, that having seizures can interrupt attention or affect memory, and this can affect the grades and school performance of people with epilepsy.

Some of the medication that is prescribed to treat epilepsy can also have this effect. Side effects from these medications, such as drowsiness, memory loss, and mood or behavior problems, can interfere with learning. For this reason, many teens with epilepsy do not like taking medication.

Treatments for seizures have also changed over time. At one time, doctors drilled holes into the skulls of people who had epilepsy in the hope that this would cure them. Other methods of treatment that have been tried over the centuries include herbs, fasting (going without food), and prayer. Today there are many medications and other treatments available to control most types of seizures.

Anyone can have a seizure. Each person has something called a seizure threshold. This is the point at which a person's brain cells will temporarily discharge bursts of irregular electrical activity. Scientists believe that we inherit our seizure threshold. No two people have exactly the same seizure threshold, however. If two people have identical brain injuries, the one with the lower seizure threshold is more likely to have a seizure. Despite the fact that seizure thresholds appear to be inherited, most people with epilepsy have no family history of the condition.

People who have epilepsy do need to make some changes in their lifestyles, but they can still lead basically normal lives. Many famous people have had epilepsy. They include the following:

- Alexander the Great
- Aristotle
- Sister Wendy Beckett
- Richard Burton
- Lord Byron
- Julius Caesar
- Lewis Carroll
- Charles Dickens

Actor Danny Glover is just one of many well-known people who have epilepsy.

- Danny Glover
- George Frideric Handel
- Joan of Arc
- James Madison
- Napoleon
- Sir Isaac Newton
- Alfred Nobel
- Edgar Allen Poe
- Socrates
- Vincent Van Gogh

18

Chapter Three

What Is Epilepsy Like?

Epilepsy, as you have learned, is a condition in which people experience seizures that are not caused by a high fever or other illness. There are at least thirty different types of seizures that people with epilepsy can experience.

Lydia is about to enter high school. There is so much to look forward to—new friends, new classes, clubs, football games, and maybe even dating. But there is also much to fear. Her friends are worrying about getting lost in the huge new school or forgetting the combination to their lockers. Lydia's fear, however, is about something else: Will she have a seizure at school?

"Why me? I want to be normal, just like every-body else," Lydia sighs.

"I had my first seizure when I was eleven years old," she says. *"I remember that Mom was nagging me to clean my room. I put on my favorite CD and turned up the volume to put me in the mood to clean. Suddenly, I felt a strange tingling in my stomach, and things got fuzzy. I don't remember anything after that. I woke up in an emergency room and didn't know what had happened."*

Lydia had had a seizure and fallen. Her parents ran to her room when they heard her fall. She was lying on the floor. Her body was stiff and her eyes were rolling up into her head. Her face was contorted, she was turning blue, and she was shaking all over. When the shaking stopped, white bubbles of saliva started coming out of her mouth. Then she abruptly started to snore and appeared to be sleeping.

At the hospital, the doctor told Lydia's parents that she would need some tests. "Mom looked pale and scared," Lydia recalls. "Dad blamed the music I had been listening to. As for me, I was so sleepy, I still didn't know what was happening.

"During the next few weeks, I made several visits to different doctors and had a bunch of tests. A month later, I had another seizure. At that point, they told me I had something called epilepsy."

Some seizures may last only a few moments and are almost imperceptible.

Ben, age fifteen, was talking to his friends about yesterday's basketball game. He suddenly stopped in midsentence. His face went blank, and he began to blink very quickly. A moment later, he was "back" with his friends and took up his sentence where he had left off. Like Lydia, Ben has epilepsy, and he had just had a seizure.

Sam describes one of his seizures this way: "I'm sitting in study hall and I begin to smell something like rotten eggs. Then everything goes black for a few seconds. Suddenly I start seeing what looks like mountains that are coming toward me. The scene stops really quickly, and I find myself still sitting in the same spot." Sam does not lose consciousness during his seizures.

High school can be stressful for all teens. Trying to fit in is a common worry, and learning and making friends are important concerns. Your interactions with your classmates and teachers during high school can have a lifelong impact. Teens with epilepsy (or any medical condition) experience even more fears and stress than teens without this condition.

"My life changed after I had my seizures," Lydia says sadly. "It started to revolve around visits to doctors and taking my medications—I am so tired of taking them! I need to get extra rest

*and sleep, and I don't know if I'll be able to keep
up with everything and everyone in high school.
What should I tell my new friends? Oh, God, I
hope I don't have a seizure in class."*

Who Gets Epilepsy?

There are 2.3 million Americans diagnosed with
epilepsy, and an estimated 50 million worldwide.
Seizures can begin at any age, but about half of all
people with epilepsy are first diagnosed when they are
under twenty-five. About one-third of people with
epilepsy are under eighteen.

People who have seizures are not sick or abnormal.
They are not retarded, crazy, or mentally ill. They look
like other people. Seizures rarely cause brain damage
or death. The only time people die during a seizure is
if the seizure does not stop or if the person dies from
an injury that occurs during a seizure, perhaps as a
result of falling or drowning. If a convulsive seizure
does not stop within five minutes or if a person has a
series of seizures one after another, it is considered a
medical emergency, and immediate medical help is
needed. This condition is called *status epilepticus,* and
it can be dangerous.

You may have heard that people can swallow their
tongues during a seizure. This is not true. People may
bite their tongue during a seizure, but they cannot

swallow it. They may also lose control of their bowels or bladder, which is embarrassing but not dangerous.

Not all seizures are convulsive, and with many types of seizures, people do not lose consciousness. Some people have seizures without knowing it. Memory gaps and periods of staring blankly can be signs of seizures, as can hearing strange sounds, having visions, mumbling, picking at clothing, experiencing muscle jerks, and suddenly having strong, unexplained sensations of fear, anger, or panic. Often it is only after someone with epilepsy notices a pattern of feelings, sensations, or behavior that he or she will seek treatment. Sometimes observers may think a person having a seizure is drunk or on drugs, and people with epilepsy have even been arrested after having a seizure.

When Amy was in second grade, her teacher noticed that Amy stared a lot while smacking her lips and fumbling with her hands. Her mother also noticed this at home. Amy's parents took her to the doctor, who gave her some tests and determined that she was having seizures. The doctor started Amy on medication. Her teacher soon reported that Amy was more alert in class, and her mother said she was less clumsy at home. If Amy had not been examined and treated, her grades might have been affected, and her behavior would have been considered "odd."

Chapter Four

Diagnosing Epilepsy

Steve was fourteen years old when he had his first seizure. He was in the garage, working on his car, when he lost consciousness. He fell to the ground and had a convulsion. Afterward, he didn't remember anything that had happened. His parents took him to the hospital, where several tests were done. All the test results were normal.

"The doctors kept asking questions. I felt as if I was getting the third degree. They asked questions like, did I remember if the garage was hot or smelly and did I feel anything strange before the seizure. They wanted to know if I had any allergies, if I was getting enough sleep, what my eating habits were like, and whether I was taking any

Doctors must rule out many possible conditions before determining if someone has epilepsy.

medications. They even asked if I used drugs! I got kind of annoyed and scared at the same time. I started to feel like I was weird or defective."

Not all seizures are indicative of epilepsy. As you now know, seizures can be caused by a variety of things, including fever, illness, and head injury. People are diagnosed with epilepsy when they experience two or more seizures when they are not ill and do not have a fever. Doctors will rule out many possible conditions before saying for certain that someone has epilepsy.

If you have had two or more seizures, you should seek medical treatment. The doctor will ask for a detailed description of exactly what happened during each seizure. Knowing if you had a headache, head injury, or jerking movements in any part of your body before the seizure will help the medical professional find the location of the irregular activity in the brain. He or she will also ask you what happened and how you felt immediately before the seizure. There will be questions about your health in general and about your family's medical history.

The reason that medical professionals ask so many questions is to learn as much as possible so that they can treat you correctly. In particular, they want to know if you have any warning that a seizure is starting. These warnings are called auras, and they may be something like a strange feeling of fear or sickness, or a sudden odd smell or taste. Sometimes people have auras without having a seizure afterward, but an aura means that some abnormal electrical activity in the brain is beginning. Sometimes this abnormal electrical activity tapers off, and at other times it spreads and leads to severe seizures.

Testing for Epilepsy

Several doctors and other health care workers may examine you. Your family doctor, pediatrician, or nurse practitioner may be the first person you meet with. Then there are specialists such as neurologists, who have received specialized training in how the brain works. The diagnosis of epilepsy relies heavily on the person's descriptions of what happened. A physical examination and several other tests will follow.

During the physical examination, the doctor or nurse practitioner will check your lungs, heart rate, blood pressure, height and weight, and the reflexes in your arms and legs, and he or she will shine a light into your eyes to check them. Then you will be given a series of tests. Blood and urine tests will be done to detect medical problems like anemia, diabetes, toxins (poisons) in the body, or kidney disease. Other tests may include an electroencephalogram (EEG), computerized tomography (CT), and magnetic resonance imaging (MRI).

The Electroencephalogram (EEG)

The EEG measures the electricity given off by brain cells. This test, which takes approximately an hour, does

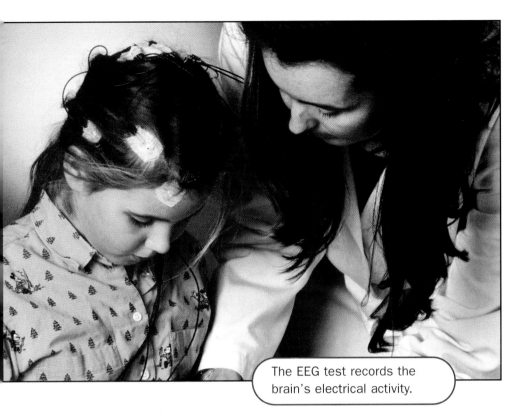

The EEG test records the brain's electrical activity.

not hurt. A technician will paste tiny wires to your head. These are connected to a machine called an electroencephalograph, which measures and records the electrical activity in the brain. The record of the activity appears on paper in wavy patterns. Sharp waves or spikes on the EEG mean that there is extra, abnormal electrical activity in the brain. If a seizure occurs during the test, the machine will record it, but the EEG does not make a diagnosis of epilepsy. Some people with epilepsy have normal EEGs, and other people can have abnormal EEGs without having epilepsy. The EEG helps the doctor determine if there is abnormal activity in a specific area of the brain and decide what treatment to recommend.

Sometimes, if there is not enough information for the doctor to make a diagnosis, a person will be attached to a portable EEG machine that measures and records brain activity for twenty-four hours to monitor any changes when the person is awake or asleep. To both see and record any seizure activity, an EEG may be combined with video monitoring. This is especially useful for people who have epilepsy but have normal EEGs.

Other Tests

The CT and MRI tests can help "see" the brain and look for abnormal structures such as tumors or enlarged blood vessels. The CT uses a low-level X ray to scan the brain, then makes a computerized picture to show abnormal structures. MRIs give an even clearer picture of the brain than CT scans. During an MRI, you must lie still for approximately forty-five minutes in a tunnel-like machine that uses a magnet to produce a picture of the brain. Additional tests may be used to measure other changes in the brain and to learn more about seizure activity. There is no single test to diagnose epilepsy. In most cases, unfortunately, none of these tests will explain the cause of someone's seizures.

"So far, they haven't found a cause for my seizures," Steve explains. "They're things that just happened. I have not had any seizures since I've been taking the medication that my doctor prescribed. I don't like having this seizure disorder or epilepsy or whatever, but I'm glad there's nothing wrong with me mentally, and I'm not contagious."

Chapter Five

Treatment

Medication is the most common treatment used to prevent and control seizures. There are many types of drugs available. They may be called different names: antiepileptic, anticonvulsant, or antiseizure drugs. We do not know how these drugs work in the brain, but they do work for most people. Currently, about 80 to 85 percent of people with epilepsy can gain control of their seizures with the proper medication. These drugs do not cure epilepsy, but they can prevent seizures from happening. It is important to learn as much about your medications as possible. Here are a few questions you should ask your doctor:

- What is the name of this medication, and is it known by any other names?

31

It is important to learn as much about your medications as possible.

- How should the medication be stored? Does it need to be kept cool or at room temperature?

- How much medication do I take, and how many times a day do I need to take it?

- Should I take the medication with food or on an empty stomach?

- What should I do if I miss a dose?

- Are there any foods or other medications that I should avoid while taking this medication?

- What are some of the common side effects that I should expect? Do I need to seek emergency medical treatment if I have any of them?

Sometimes people have to take more than one type of antiseizure drug in order to control their seizures. Other medications, including acne medications, antibiotics, and even some over-the-counter drugs, may interfere with the effectiveness of antiseizure drugs. Be sure to tell your doctor if you are taking any other drugs.

It can be difficult to find the right medication and the correct dose because everyone's body reacts somewhat differently to medication. A certain amount of the antiseizure drug has to stay in your body for it to control your seizures. Your doctor measures this amount by taking samples of your blood.

Tony, age seventeen, explains, "I was on one medication for four months. The side effects got so bad that I had to be gradually taken off that one and started on another. I was seizure-free for one month, but the doctor had to increase the dose, and I developed an allergy to that medication. I had to start a third one. It was so frustrating. I thought the doctor would never get my medication right!"

Medication and Side Effects

Many different antiseizure drugs are available. Various things will help your doctor determine which medication to prescribe. These include the following:

- Your age
- Any drug allergies you might have

- The type of seizures you have had
- The side effects of the drug
- The cost of the drug

Side effects can be mild or severe. If you notice side effects from your medication, it is important to write down what you are experiencing and discuss it with your doctor. Some common side effects are increased appetite, irritability, nausea, drowsiness, hyperactivity, and difficulty remembering things. Changing the dose of an antiseizure drug or switching to another type of drug will often eliminate side effects. Before changing your medication, your doctor will check your blood levels and ask you about any seizures you have had while on the medication.

Some of the behavioral side effects of antiseizure medication can make it hard to tell the difference between normal teenage behavior and a side effect of medication. Many teens, for example, are frequently sleepy because their growing bodies need more sleep than their busy lives allow them to get. However, lack of sleep can be dangerous for a teenager with epilepsy because it can cause seizures.

In most cases, epilepsy does not need to be treated forever. Doctors cannot predict who will continue to have seizures and who will not. Some people simply outgrow their epilepsy. If a patient with epilepsy has not had a seizure for two years, the doctor may gradually stop the antiseizure medication. Use of antiseizure drugs must be tapered off slowly and not stopped abruptly, or else a seizure may occur. Never stop taking your medication on your own. Your doctor may slowly take you off medication during the summer so that there is no risk that you will have a seizure at school.

Other Treatments

There are other treatments for epilepsy besides medication. Surgery, diet, and a surgically implanted device are some of the other options. These may be more appropriate for you, depending on the type of seizures you have.

Surgery

Surgery may be used when the activity that causes seizures is located in an area of the brain where surgery can be performed safely—an area that does not control an important function such as speech or memory. The surgeon will remove damaged cells or a tumor or other growth that may be causing seizures. Even if surgery is successful and the abnormality is safely and completely removed, the person may still have seizures. All surgery has serious risks, even in relatively safe areas of the brain, that must be taken into consideration before surgery is recommended. Your doctor will tell you if an operation is a possibility for you.

Ketogenic Diet

Some doctors have tried prescribing a special diet called a ketogenic diet to treat seizures that cannot be controlled by medication. This diet involves fasting, then eating foods that are high in fat and low in protein and carbohydrates. This creates a condition called ketosis. It is believed that chemicals that the body produces in ketosis may act to control seizures. The diet is hard to stay on, and people cannot go off it suddenly or without a doctor's supervision.

Vagus Nerve Stimulators

Implanting a device called a vagus nerve stimulator is a relatively new method of treating epilepsy. The vagus nerve stimulator is a small device that is implanted under the skin in the person's chest. It sends small electrical signals to the vagus nerve, which is the largest nerve in the body. It is programmed to control the pattern of your brain waves and can help prevent seizures.

Epilepsy is a highly treatable condition. In addition to the many treatments already available, researchers are working on new ways to diagnose brain abnormalities as well as new drugs and techniques to control seizures and provide hope for the future.

Chapter Six

Special Concerns for Teenagers

*J*im, sixteen, was sent to Mr. Oko in the guidance office for being "disruptive" in class.

Jim does not recall being disruptive in class. He remembers watching Ms. Wilson solve a problem on the chalkboard. The next thing he knew, he was being escorted out of the classroom. Ms. Wilson said that Jim started banging on his desk and walking around the room. When she told him to return to his seat, Jim looked straight at her and ignored her.

Jim's grades had been dropping all year. He was failing one subject and barely passing two others. In the past, he had always been a good student, and he had never failed a class before.

Jim was very polite as he talked to Mr. Oko, even though he seemed tired and answered questions

Teens with epilepsy are often forbidden by their parents to drive.

slowly. Mr. Oko learned that Jim had had seizures when he was in second grade and had not been to the doctor in several years.

Mr. Oko called Jim's mother. She agreed to take Jim to a doctor and to report Jim's problems in school. The doctor learned that Jim was having seizures, and she prescribed medication.

By the end of the school year, Jim was able to pass all of his courses, and Ms. Wilson gained an understanding of seizures.

Most people have never witnessed a seizure. Learning more about seizures can help to lessen fears. People need to learn that seizures are a temporary condition of the brain and that they are not contagious.

Many people would probably like to know how to help someone who is having a seizure.

Teens with epilepsy are often concerned about how the condition will affect them at school—about how epilepsy might affect their grades and social life, and what their classmates will think of them. One of their most common fears is having a seizure in front of others. They worry that they will be horribly embarrassed if they space out, shout, fall down, shake, foam at the mouth, or urinate or defecate—any of which can happen during a seizure. Many do not want to return to school after having had a seizure there.

No one needs to isolate him- or herself if he or she has seizures. It is helpful for teens with epilepsy to talk to others about their condition and share their concerns with friends, family members, classmates, and teachers.

Epilepsy and Driving

Getting a driver's license is a major goal for most teens. Students with epilepsy should not be excluded from the school's driver education programs. State laws vary in how long a person has to be seizure-free before being permitted to drive, but all students should take the classroom instruction portion of the course. The information given in these classes is important, and taking the class may reduce the cost of insurance premiums when the teen gets his or her license.

Susan wants to be able to drive, just like all of her friends. Most of them know that Susan has epilepsy and cannot drive, but it is still hard for her to be different. She often gets annoyed with her parents for fussing over her, and having one of them drive her everywhere only makes things worse.

"Mom is always asking me if I've remembered to take my medication," Susan sighs. "I don't want to take it, but I really don't want to have another seizure. I want to drive. I know my parents are worried that if I learn to drive, I'll have a seizure and get into an accident. But I still wish they wouldn't nag me. It's bugging me. I wish my epilepsy would just go away."

Activities and Classes

Students with epilepsy should be able to participate safely in physical education class and athletics unless their doctors tell them to restrict certain activities. Vigorous physical activity is not associated with an increase in seizures. People with epilepsy should be supervised or accompanied by nonepileptic friends during certain activities, such as swimming and climbing, that could result in serious injury if a seizure occurred. At school, gym staff should be notified if there are students with epilepsy in their classes, and they should be instructed about what to look for and how to manage a seizure if one occurs. Safety is a concern in all school programs, and that includes courses such as shop as well as physical education.

Some teens with epilepsy also have learning problems.

Most high school students worry about their grades. Teens with epilepsy may worry even more about academic performance if they also have learning problems. Such learning problems include being unable to stay focused on work, having trouble following directions, and missing things that the teacher says. This can be because of the epilepsy itself or the effects of antiseizure medications. Some students with epilepsy get help from special education services or extra tutoring. Others benefit from techniques such as writing lists of things to remember or reviewing audio cassettes or videotapes of lessons. Keeping a journal can also be an effective way to remember things, and families can also help with reminders. If you have epilepsy, remember to tell your doctor about any problems you are having in school.

Epilepsy and Your Family

Parents can be overprotective. They may worry about your safety if you take part in various school activities. They may ask you the same questions again and again: Did you take your medication? How do you feel? Are you having any unusual symptoms? Remember that your parents mean well and care about you. They wish for you to be seizure-free, and they want only what is best for you. They also worry about your future.

Good communication with your parents can help them worry less about you. Ask them to help you try to make your high school years more enjoyable by working with your school to allow you to participate in school activities and get any extra help you need. They can also help you plan for college or a career.

Occasionally epilepsy—or the medication used to treat it—may cause behavior problems in teenagers. It is important for these teens to work with their parents, their doctors, and other concerned adults to resolve any behavior problems. If the problems include mood changes, feelings of isolation and low self-esteem, or depression, a psychologist, psychiatrist, or other mental health professional may be able to help.

If you feel that epilepsy is creating emotional or behavioral problems for you, sharing your concerns with family, teachers, school guidance counselors, and school nurses can help you to solve these problems. Support from these people and others can be very valuable. The people you speak with may be able to help you find others with epilepsy who share your concerns and problems. The Epilepsy Foundation of America (EFA) offers a wealth of information such as books, videos, and pamphlets. This organization and others like it can help answer your questions, provide services, and organize support groups to help you. The EFA even sponsors an Internet chat room for teens. Check the back of this book for organizations and Web sites that can get you started.

Your siblings can also be a source of support. Remember to talk to your brothers or sisters about your epilepsy. Encourage them to ask questions about the condition and to share their feelings about having a brother or sister with epilepsy. Everyone will gain support and understanding.

Concerns About the Future

When Carol was twelve, her body started to change. She grew three inches in one year, gained twenty pounds, grew pubic hair, developed breasts, began using antiperspirant, and got her first period. She spent lots of time admiring herself in the mirror and experimenting with different hairstyles. There was nothing she wanted more than to hang out with her friends. All of this was normal for a girl Carol's age. But at this same time, unlike most girls her age, Carol was diagnosed with epilepsy.

Today Carol is fifteen, and her seizures have been controlled with medication. She has been able to lead

It is important to talk honestly with your siblings about your epilepsy.

a mostly normal life as a teenager. She has taken medication three times a day for the past three years. Because of the medication, she never even thinks about using drugs or drinking. She leads a healthy lifestyle and makes sure she gets enough sleep.

"When I first started to take my medication, the doctor needed to measure my blood level every two or three weeks," Carol says. "I didn't like having my blood drawn, and going to the doctor so often took up a lot of my time. Now my blood level is checked only once or twice a year. I don't like taking the medication—it has a few side effects—but it is way better than having seizures."

Carol keeps a journal, and she noticed that when she used to have frequent seizures, they always occurred around the time of her periods. This happens to a lot of girls and women with epilepsy, although no one is sure why. Keeping a journal is a good idea for many people, but it can be especially helpful for girls who have a seizure disorder.

Carol has other concerns. She wonders if she will be able to date, get married, and have children someday. The answer to all three questions is yes.

Most teenagers want to date. Everyone wants to find someone special to love. Beginning to date will be a new experience for you—and also for your parents. To make it easier, try to talk to them about your concerns and ask them about theirs. Discussing things in advance can help prevent many problems when you start to date.

It is smart to tell your date about your epilepsy. Many people have misconceptions about seizures, and talking about epilepsy will help relieve some of your anxiety as well as theirs. Your date should also know what to do in case you have a seizure.

Alcohol and drugs can cause seizures in anyone. These substances have special risks for people who take antiseizure medication because of the way that drugs and alcohol interact with the medication. If you want confidential information about the risks of alcohol and drugs for epileptics, you can contact the Epilepsy Foundation of America.

If you are a teen with epilepsy and you are sexually active, be aware of the risks of date rape, the need to practice safe sex, and the proper use of birth control methods. Girls should know that antiseizure medications can interfere with the effectiveness of birth control pills, thereby putting them at greater risk of pregnancy.

Many girls and women with epilepsy wonder if they will be able to have children. In almost all cases, they can if a doctor carefully monitors their health during the pregnancy. There is some risk to a developing fetus from antiseizure medications, and any woman with epilepsy who is thinking about getting pregnant should discuss this with her health care provider first.

New mothers who have epilepsy need to plan how they can safely care for their babies in case they have a seizure. Children of parents who have epilepsy should learn safety procedures in case their parents have a seizure. Even very young children can be taught to call 911 if a parent has a seizure.

Life After High School

Growing up requires people to accept more responsibility. This includes taking responsibility for your medications, your health, and your actions. Doing well in school and preparing for the future are things to think about.

Many people with epilepsy go on to college. Others choose to work after high school. Talk to your guidance counselor about planning for life after high school. Talk to career counselors, advisors, and prospective employers about different jobs and careers. People with epilepsy are employed in a wide range of jobs, and many are very successful.

The Americans with Disabilities Act (ADA) of 1992 makes it illegal for employers to discriminate against people with medical disabilities. However, there are some jobs that people with epilepsy cannot perform. These include piloting commercial airliners and working as long-haul truckers. The Epilepsy Foundation of America can offer guidance and information about employment and careers for people with epilepsy.

Chapter Seven

Prevention and First Aid

It is important to know as much about your epilepsy as possible. Make sure you know what type of seizures you have and whether they are caused by anything in particular. Things that may cause you to have a seizure are called triggers. There are many types of triggers.

One common trigger is forgetting to take antiseizure medication. It can be hard to remember to take your medication at the same time every day. Some medications have unpleasant side effects that can make you reluctant to take them. If this happens, don't skip your medication—keep taking it until you can talk to your doctor about how to get rid of the side effects. Teens often think that if they have not had a seizure recently, they no longer need their medication. Remember, though, that the medication controls the seizures and that it is not safe to suddenly stop taking your medication. Other triggers may include:

- Lack of sleep
- Stress
- Flashing lights such as strobe lights
- Extreme hot or cold
- Certain video games
- Substances such as alcohol and caffeine

Sleep is essential for everyone, but when a person with epilepsy does not get enough sleep, a seizure often results. Good eating habits are also important for everyone, but when a person with epilepsy skips meals, the drop in the body's blood sugar can trigger a seizure. In general, a healthy lifestyle can help to keep you seizure-free. Teenagers are old enough to be responsible for taking their medication, getting enough sleep, and eating properly. Sharing this information with your friends will help them understand your needs.

Telling Your Friends About Epilepsy

Most teens would prefer to forget or ignore their epilepsy. Unfortunately, that will not help at all. Instead, teens with epilepsy must take control of the disorder rather than letting it control them.

If you feel a seizure coming on, stop what you are doing and, if possible, get to a safe place.

It is very important to tell your friends that you have epilepsy. Most likely, they will want to know how they can help you if you have a seizure. If you are aware of an aura before you have a seizure, you can prepare yourself for the seizure by heading to a safe place and telling someone what is about to happen. If you don't get auras, your friends can still help once a seizure starts by watching out for your safety.

Tell your friends what epilepsy is and what happens to you when you have a seizure. Seizures with convulsions can look very frightening, so make sure your friends know that these seizures are neither painful nor life threatening. Don't worry about losing your friends because of your epilepsy. True friends like you just as you are. Your real friends will want to be your friends whether or not you have epilepsy. Be sure to tell them what to do if you have a convulsive seizure.

If someone feels a seizure coming on, he or she should tell someone. Others can help the person stay safe during the seizure and stay with him or her until it is over. If you are alone and you feel a seizure coming on, you can take some precautions. For example, if you are riding your bike, stop and get off; if you are driving, pull over to the side of the road.

Many people, however, cannot tell when they are about to have a seizure. For these people, wearing a Medic Alert bracelet or necklace is a good idea. This states that you have a seizure disorder. Some Medic Alert bracelets also list the name of your medication and the phone number of a parent or other emergency contact.

First Aid for Seizures

Convulsive seizures require first aid. If you see someone having a convulsive seizure, here are the steps you should take:

- ◆ Clear any objects that are in the way so that the person does not hurt himself or herself when his or her muscles jerk.

- ◆ If possible, turn the person on his or her side so that there is no risk that he or she will choke on saliva.

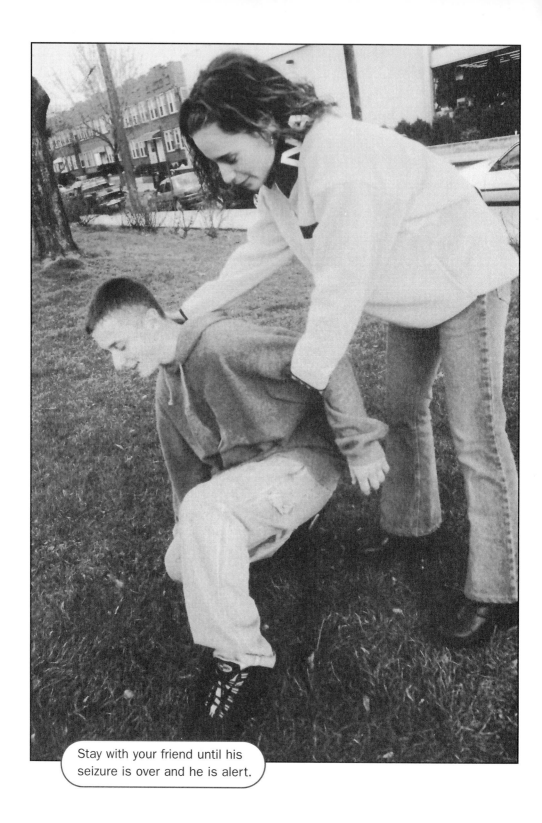

Stay with your friend until his seizure is over and he is alert.

- Loosen ties, collars, scarves, or other items around the neck to prevent choking.

- If the person wears glasses, remove them if possible.

- If the person kicks or flails the arms or legs, do not attempt to restrain him or her.

- Stay with the person until the seizure is over and he or she is awake and alert. After a seizure, a person with epilepsy may be briefly confused, disoriented, or sleepy.

Complex partial seizures may also require help, though simple partial seizures do not require first aid. As with convulsive seizures, you should not try to restrain a person who is having a complex partial seizure. Just remove any objects in the person's way and stay with him or her until the seizure stops.

> *Kevin plays varsity basketball. At the beginning of the season, he tells his teammates about his epilepsy. "Epilepsy is a condition in which seizures happen," he tells them. "Seizures are short malfunctions of the brain's electrical system. They are not contagious, and most can be controlled with medication.*
>
> *"There are two major types of seizures—those with convulsions and those without convulsions. Some people have both types, but I get convulsive seizures. They can look pretty frightening, but*

they don't hurt, and I can't remember them after they happen.

"When I have a seizure, I usually yell kind of loud and fall to the ground. My eyes roll up, and my body gets very stiff. Sometimes my face turns red and my lips get a little bluish. My body starts jerking, and I sometimes drool. The seizure usually lasts about two minutes. When it's over, I am achy all over and usually sleep for a while. My brain and body need a rest after all that activity."

"Is there anything we can do to keep you from having a seizure?" Kevin's teammate Jason asks.

"No," Kevin replies. "Once the seizure starts, there's nothing anyone can do. Just try to clear the area so I don't hurt myself on anything. If I'm wearing a tie or if anything else is wrapped around my neck, try to loosen it. If possible, try to put something soft under my head, like a jacket or sweater. You can take my glasses off if I'm wearing them so that they don't break. If you can, roll me onto my side so that the saliva drips out of my mouth and doesn't choke me. I know the whole thing sounds gross, but you guys are my friends, and I don't want you to be afraid or flipped out if I have a seizure."

Jamal asks if the coach should call the paramedics if Kevin has a seizure.

"If the seizure lasts more than five minutes, or if I have one seizure after another, then call

them," Kevin answers. "Otherwise, there is nothing they can do. The best thing you guys can do is stay with me until the seizure is over and I wake up. Then you can tell me all about it!"

His teammates tell him that they want to help and that they will do all they can for him.

Kevin has also explained to his friends that he cannot drive yet. His friends offer him rides and help him make sure that he gets home from parties at a reasonable hour so that he gets enough sleep. They accept him and understand that just as their friend Jim has asthma and Paul has diabetes, Kevin has epilepsy. They know that it doesn't make him different in any way that matters.

Glossary

aura   A feeling or other sensation that some people with epilepsy have right before a seizure.

complex partial seizure   A type of seizure that affects only part of the brain. This type of seizure causes a person to move strangely, pick at clothing, or exhibit other unusual behavior, but does not lead to convulsions. The person has no memory of what happened during the seizure.

computerized tomography (CT)   A type of medical test that provides a three-dimensional image of the area being examined. CT scans are used to examine the brains of people with epilepsy.

concussion   An injury to the head that can cause seizures.

convulsion   A violent, uncontrollable movement of the body's muscles, with loss of consciousness.

electroencephalogram (EEG)   A type of medical test that measures and records electrical activity in the brain.

generalized seizure   A type of seizure that affects the entire brain.

ketogenic diet   A diet high in fat and low in carbohydrates and protein that some experts believe can reduce the occurrence of seizures.

magnetic resonance imaging (MRI)   A type of medical test that gives a clear picture of the area being examined.

seizure   A temporary period of abnormal electrical activity in the brain.

seizure threshold   The point at which a person's brain cells will produce irregular electrical activity.

simple partial seizure   A type of seizure that affects only part of the brain. Muscles and senses may be affected. People who have simple partial seizures usually remember them afterward.

status epilepticus   A seizure that lasts a long time or the occurrence of two or more seizures one after another. The person does not regain consciousness and requires emergency treatment.

trigger   Any event or occurrence that may bring on a seizure.

vagus nerve stimulator   A device that is implanted in the chest and helps control brain activity to prevent seizures.

Where to Go for Help

In the United States

Epilepsy Foundation of America (EFA)
4351 Garden City Drive, Suite 406
Landover, MD 20785
(800) EFA-1000 [332-1000]
Web site: http://www.efa.org
E-mail: postmaster@efa.org
Teen chat room: http://www.teenchat.org

The Epilepsy Institute
257 Park Avenue
New York, NY 10019
(212) 677-8550
Web site: http://www.alz2.com

National Epilepsy Hotline
(800) 642-0500 or (919) 748-2319

In Canada

Epilepsy Canada
1470 Peel Street, Suite 745
Montreal, PQ H3A 1T1
(514) 845-7866
Web site: http://www.epilepsy.ca

Epilepsy Ontario
1 Promenade Circle, Suite 308
Thornhill, ON M4J 4P8
(800) 463-1119
(416) 229-2291
Web site: http://www.epilepsyontario.org

For Further Reading

Bergman, Thomas. *Moments That Disappear: Children Living with Epilepsy*. Milwaukee: Gareth Stevens, 1992.

Carson, Mary Kay. *Epilepsy*. Springfield, NJ: Enslow Publishers, 1998.

Devinsky, Orrin. *A Guide to Understanding and Living with Epilepsy*. Philadelphia, PA: F.A. Davis Co., 1994.

Dudley, Mark E. *Epilepsy*. Parsippany, NJ: Crestwood House, 1998.

Epilepsy Foundation. *Issues and Answers: Exploring Your Possibilities: A Guide for Teens and Young Adults with Epilepsy.* Landover, MD: Epilepsy Foundation of America, 1992.

Landau, Elaine. *Epilepsy*. New York: Twenty-First Century Books, 1994.

McGowen, Tom. *Epilepsy*. New York: Franklin Watts, 1989.

Richard, Adrienne, and Joel Reiter. *Epilepsy: A New Approach*. New York: Walker and Company, 1995.

Schachter, Steven C. *Brainstorms: Epilepsy in Our Words*. New York: Raven Press, 1994.

_____. *The Brainstorms Family: Epilepsy on Our Terms*. New York: Raven Press, 1996.

Index

Index

About the Author

Patricia Emanuele, R.N., has a master's degree in nursing and experience working with adults and children. She is a health educator and school nurse who is committed to promoting health and wellness. She has written health education materials; this is her first book for young readers. She lives in Metuchen, New Jersey.

Photo Credits

Cover and pp. 2, 12, 14, 21, 26, 32, 38, 41, 44, 50, 52 by Bob Van Lindt; pp. 6, 29 © Custom Medical; p. 18 © Everett Collection.

Layout Design

Michael J. Caroleo